From the best selling author of "The Order of Melchizedek!"

PERSONAL TRANSFORMATION CLINIC

*...A Cutting Edge School of Ministry
on Personal Transformation
Student Training Manual*

By Dr. Francis Myles
Chancellor

www.francismyles.com   Copyrights Reserved 2014

ORDER OF MELCHIZEDEK

LEADERSHIP UNIVERSITY

CONTACT:
Pastor Suzette Torti
Phone. 0421 353 361
Email info@openheaven.org.au

www.openheaven.org.au

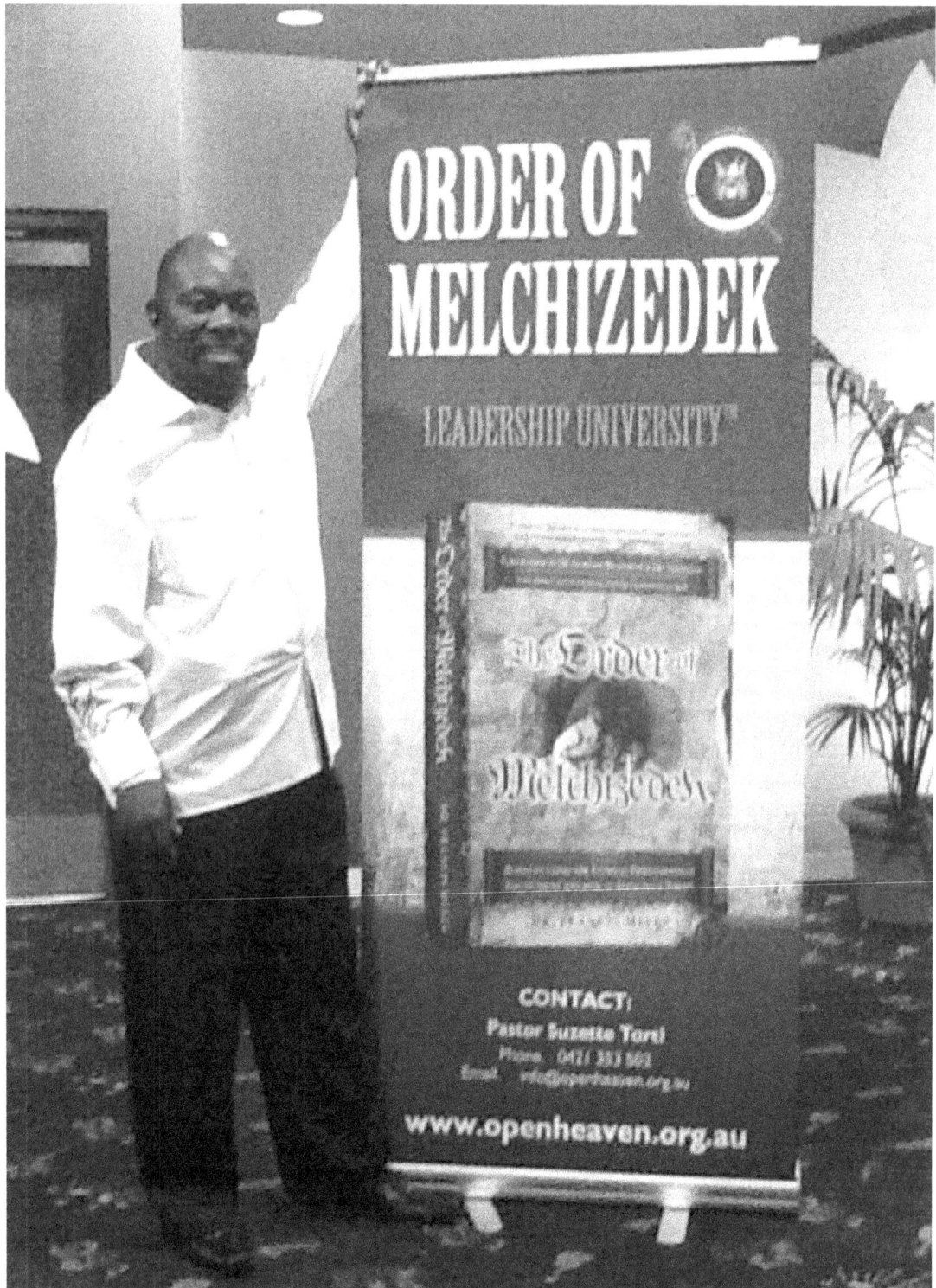

Table of Contents

FIRST WORD...MESSAGE
FROM THE CHANCELLOR

The Beginning....

When I wrote the book the Order of Melchizedek, I deeply underestimated the level of hunger that existed in the Body of Christ for a book about an ancient priestly order that has present day ramifications for followers of Christ who are tired of church as usual or knowing Christ "the image of the invisible God" from a religiously safe distance. By far my biggest shock came from seeing how many marketplace leaders and ministers (businessmen and women) went into a frenzy of delight when they got a copy of the book. Within months of this book's release many businessmen and women were affectionately calling the "The Order of Melchizedek" their "Marketplace Bible." Things quickly went over the top for me when pastors joined marketplace leaders in celebrating this book. One great man of God who presides over 200 churches, told me that "The Order of Melchizedek" is the best book that he has ever read in 40 years of active ministry!

The Vision....

After the first printing of the book "The Order of Melchizedek" God gave me a vision of what He intended to do with this book around the world. But I know that God never does anything unless it is already finished. I knew that God was calling me to be part of manifesting here on earth a "finished work" from "Eternity-past" concerning the supernatural establishment of the Order of Melchizedek on our troubled planet. In this vision I saw myself standing on a map of the seven continents. Suddenly pockets of "red lights" began to appear on the seven continents. While I looked a white beam of light began to join the red dots together and suddenly I saw it. A net or a matrix of red and white lights had covered the seven continents. I said to the Lord, "Lord what is this?"

The Answer...

"Son, the red lights are men and women whom I have been preparing to have a ministry that is patterned after the Order of Melchizedek. The white light that was connecting the red dots is the revelation that I have placed in your book. The revelation that I have given you will become the catalyst that will unite this global movement of my people who are waking up to the fact that I have called them to be "Kings and Priests" in the earth.

The Problem....

I was in Tulsa, Oklahoma to meet with publishers who wanted to take the "Order of Melchizedek" nationwide and then worldwide. After a successful meeting with these potential investors....the Lord dropped a word into my spirit that put everything in perspective. He told me that He wanted to take this message around the world like He had promised me, but HE DID NOT WANT ME TO LIMIT HIM, by thinking that I was going to single handedly carry this very important message to the global Body of Christ. God told me that He wanted me to "duplicate myself" in other faithful men and women who can also teach others. The Lord said to me "Son, as this message explodes around the world you will start getting an abundance of ministry invitations; I do not want you to turn down invitations without giving my people an alternative minister who can go and teach on the Order of Melchizedek in your absence." This instruction and conversation from the Lord weighed deeply upon my spirit!

The Confirmation...

A couple hours after the Lord spoke to me, I got a phone call that made it absolutely clear that the Lord had spoken to me about duplicating myself so that the message on the "Order of Melchizedek" could spread beyond my personal capacity to travel. Two very astute businessmen from Northwest Arkansas called me and this is what they told me... "Dr. Myles we feel like the message that God has given you will also become our life message but even though we are very excited about it, we feel ill equipped. We want to be able to explain the "Order of Melchizedek" with as much clarity and passion as you do. We would like to come and spend a weekend with you, so you can pour all that you have into our lives!" I was both speechless and excited....God had cornered me into a no-retreat-position.

The Solution...

On my drive back from Tulsa, I prayed earnestly. During my time of prayer the Holy Spirit gave me the solution. He told me that "Son, the spirit of a Judge is upon you NOW! I have given you the power to "Summon" my people from all walks of life to come and be "judged" concerning their understanding and compliance with the Order of Melchizedek. Call them NOW...and they will come."

The Birth of a Leadership Training University...

The Holy Spirit showed me how to set up a very intimate, prophetic and intensive Training Institute that would train "Kingdom citizens, especially marketplace leaders" how to operate under the Order of Melchizedek as "Kings and Priests." This intimate time of ministry and training will usually take place, one weekend a month. "Invited students" or "Registered Students" start class on Wednesday or Thursday and Graduate on Saturday. The name that the Holy Spirit gave me for this "one of a kind school of ministry" is "The Order of Melchizedek Leadership University" also known as "The Order of Melchizedek Leadership Institute and Seminary."

Once you are registered..

You will receive a "Welcome and Orientation Letter and Email" from Institute Chancellor. This welcome and orientation letter will acquaint you with "Leadership University Protocols, Requirements and Class Schedule."

Tuition Fees....

The Order of Melchizedek Leadership Institute and Seminary is NOT yet a "Tuition" based institute, instead we charge registration fees. Registration fees vary from school to school, especially as we add more courses to our offering. The only other expenses that you will incur are lodging, meals and travel. The tuition or registration fees cover the following...your "Student Manual" and your "Graduation Certificate."

Offerings of Honor...

Since the "Order of Melchizedek Leadership University" or OMLU is NOT a tuition based institute; students are asked to come "prayerful" about "Sowing Free Will Offerings of Honor" into the life and ministry of the Chancellor before the Saturday morning graduation service.

The Alumni....

Graduating students will be given an opportunity to "JOIN" the "Order of Melchizedek Alumni Association." This is an online community of "Melchizedeks" (men and women who are graduates of OMLU) who are operating as "Kings and Priests" both in the temple and in the marketplace. To join this community email "info@francismyles.com." You will have an opportunity to create some very meaningful relationships with men and women of "like precious faith" who are "SOLD OUT to CHRIST!"

Yours for Kingdom Advancement

Dr. Francis Myles
Chancellor

ORDER *of* **MELCHIZEDEK**
LEADERSHIP UNIVERSITY

STUDENT INFO:

Name: _____

Address: _____

City: _____ State: _____ Zip: _____

Email: _____

Tel: _____

Church Affiliation: _____

If lost please return this manual to the above address

THE ORDER OF MELCHIZEDEK ALUMNI ASSOCIATION

Graduating students will be given an opportunity to "JOIN" the "Order of Melchizedek Alumni Association." This is an online community of "Melchizedeks" (men and women who are graduates of the Order of Melchizedek Leadership Institute & Seminary) who are operating as "Kings and Priests" in the temple and in the marketplace. Simply email us at "info@francismyles.com." You will have an opportunity to create some very meaningful relationships with men and women of "like precious faith" who are "SOLD OUT to CHRIST!"

LEADERSHIP UNIVERSITY OBJECTIVES

❖ Transform ordinary believers into CMVP's = "Christ's Most Valuable Players."

❖ To create a platform for "Total Transformation" for men and women who are called to be "Josephs and Daniels" in the Marketplace

❖ To "train and raise" an end-time dominion minded company of men and women who have a ministry that is patterned after the "Order of Melchizedek" (A King-priest Ministry)

❖ To train Pastors who desire to "Introduce their Congregation to the Order of Melchizedek."

❖ To CHANGE the WORLD...one person at a time!

STUDENT EXERCISES

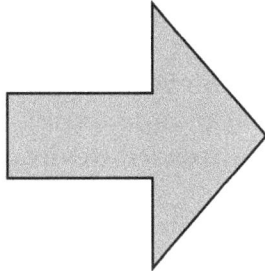

1: IN SEARCH OF VISION

Where there is no vision, the people perish: but he that keepeth the law, happy is he. Proverbs 29:18

REVIEW AND REFLECT:

Take a few moments NOW to read the following nuggets of wisdom.

"Frustration with the Present Creates the Future" by Mike Murdock

"The Flowers of Tomorrow are hidden in the Seeds of Today"..Unknown Philosopher

"Empty your wallet into your mind and your mind will fill your wallet" by Benjamin Franklin

"Jesus Christ is the Kingdom of God putting on Flesh and then Walking" Stanley E Jones

WHY SEARCH FOR YOUR VISION?

- Your Vision is an image of the future that you desire that inspires you to work towards its fulfillment.

- Your Vision inspires you to break away from your Comfort Zone into the faith world of the unknown.

- When you do not have a Vision you are easily distracted by every demonic scheme that is designed to rob you of your focus.

- Your Vision is an important portrait of your future.

- When you have a clear and well defined Vision it informs all the decisions that you make.

Consider these facts...

❖ A Vision engages your heart and your regenerated spirit

❖ A Vision expresses your deepest desire for yourself and your loved ones

❖ A Vision provides meaning to the Work or Study that you are doing

❖ A Vision is the release of unexpressed desires or dreams

❖ A Vision often expresses your desire for a "more excellent standard" of living and personal accomplishments

Make your Vision so powerful that each time you revisit it in your mind; you get deeply moved to an unshakeable course of action. We want you to create in a few minutes a clear cut Vision of what you desire to accomplish in your life by going through "The Order of Melchizedek School of Ministry."

EXPLORE AND ASSIMILATE:

Through the following exercises, you have the opportunity to create a vision for your life. We are going to ask you to take a few minutes and prayerfully meditate and answer the following questions...these questions are designed to set your creative spirit free to DREAM and DREAM BIG....

Go beyond your current life circumstances. See past what you are currently going through and picture your ideal life in the Kingdom of God.

YOUR QUEST FOR VISION:

Please answer the following questions:

1. What would I like to do in my life if I knew that I could never fail?

_____

_____

_____

_____

_____

2. At the end of my life what will be my greatest accomplishment?

_____

_____

_____

_____

_____

3. What mission in life absolutely inspires me to action?

_____

_____

_____

_____

_____

4. What are I am going to do to change the world with my understanding of the Order of Melchizedek?

_____

_____

_____

_____

_____

5. What work do I find absorbing and engaging?

_____

_____

_____

_____

_____

2. FINDING YOUR BIG WHY?

?

REVIEW AND REFLECT

The purpose of this section is to help you ESTABLISH three very important things before going through the "Order of Melchizedek Leadership University Modules."

i.   We want to help you CONNECT with your BIG WHY?

ii. We want to help you DEFINE your CORE BELIEFS

iii. We want to help you HONOR your VISION and PURPOSE for coming to the Order of Melchizedek Leadership Center "Weekend Encounter."

WHY DISCOVER YOUR BIG WHY?

Your "Big Why" is your deep emotional and spiritual reason for wanting to enhance your walk with God by attending the Order of Melchizedek Leadership University "School of Ministry." Your "Big Why" connects your presence for being in this class to your life Vision. Your "Big Why" is your connection to what God desires to do with you to advance His Kingdom here on earth.

Your "Big Why" motivates you to achieve your goals and dreams. When you know your strongest reasons for attending the Order of Melchizedek Leadership University "School of Ministry" you will easily stay on track during the rest of this weekend class modules.

Without a "Big Why"- you will lack a clear vision of how your graduating from the Order of Melchizedek Leadership University contributes to the building of the life that you have desired for yourself.

When you are aware of your "Big Why", you make better choices everyday and are able to stay the course. You expend your energy developing the kind of relationships and businesses that make your heart sing and shout!

Module

1

THE WAR ON CONSCIOUSNESS

Behold, I am with you and will keep you wherever you go, and will bring you back to this land; for I will not leave you until I have done what I have spoken to you." 16Then Jacob awoke from his sleep and said, "Surely the Lord is in this place, and I did not know it" (Genesis 28:15-16, NKJV).

Module OVERVIEW:

In this module we will answer the following questions:

1. What is the War on _____?

2. Why is the _____ the most important _____ of our time?

3. How can Consciousness help you relate to the _____ of the Living God?

4. _____ and _____ are the diseases of our modern age?

Important points to remember in this Module:

- There are forces seen and unseen in the world we live in that are engaged in an ongoing and calculated assault on the subject of "Consciousness" as it relates to knowing the person of God.

- At the frontlines of this assault on "Consciousness" are some unsuspecting members of the New Age movement, who refer to Consciousness as an elevated sense of personal enlightenment.

- Consciousness, which does not lead us into the outstretched arms of a loving God, is no Consciousness at all, but a deceptive blanket of darkness. And do not marvel; for Satan himself is transformed into an angel of light (2 Corinthians 11:14, KJV).

- "The enemy always tries to mirror everything that God is doing. In order to get a lie to be believed, it has to be very close to the truth, or close to an exact replica with a slight twist - just enough to be turned sideways.

- Consciousness is the aspect of you that will increase and grow so that your strength and purity, with the help of God, might increase. Without consciousness, you cannot really see or obey any of the real laws that are for your protection.

IMPORTANT DIAGRAMS

Figure: 1

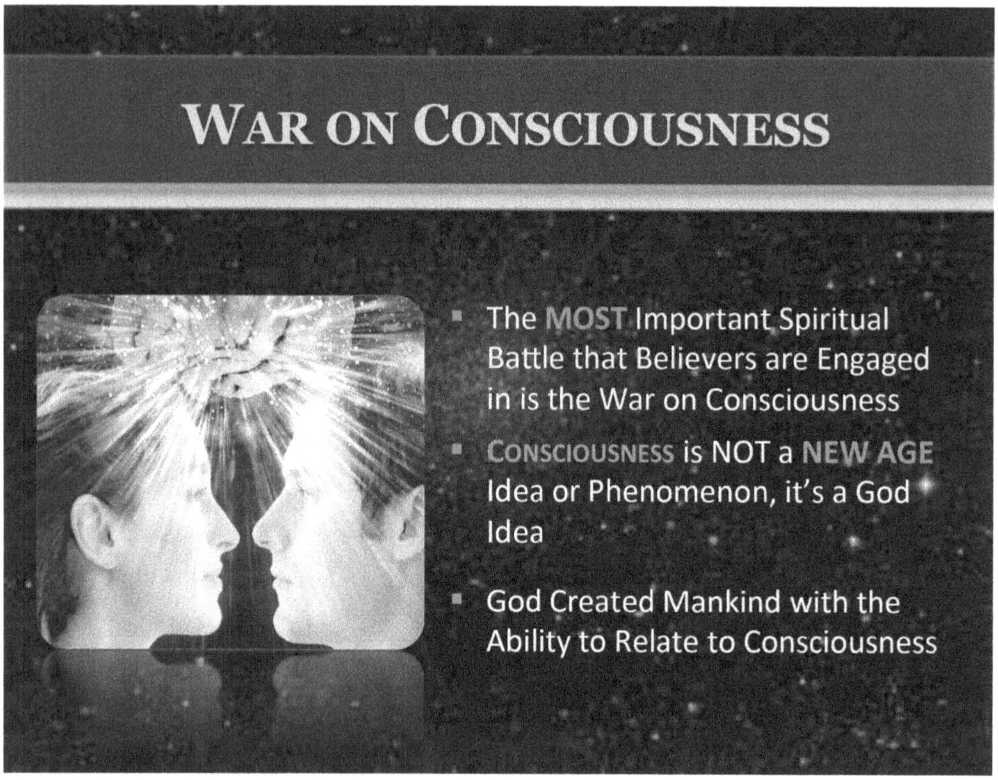

Figure: 2

Student Class Notes:

Module
2
DEFINING CONSCIOUSNESS

MEMORY VERSE

Jesus said, "At my Father's direction I have done many good works. For which one are you going to stone me?" 33They replied, "We're stoning you not for any good work, but for blasphemy! You, a mere man, claim to be God." 34Jesus replied, "It is written in your own Scriptures that God said to certain leaders of the people, 'I say, you are gods!' 35And you know that the Scriptures cannot be altered. So if those people who received God's message were called 'gods,' 36why do you call it blasphemy when I say, 'I am the Son of God'? After all, the Father set me apart and sent me into the world (John 10:32-36).

Module OVERVIEW:

In this module we will answer the following questions:

1. Why the _____ wanted to _____ for saying that He was the Son of God?

2. What are the _____ of the _____ of the Holy Spirit?

3. What is the role of the _____ in establishing _____?

4. Why is the Holy Spirit referred to as the _____?

Important points to remember on this Module:

- Stripped of "consciousness" by demonic powers, many people have forgotten that they have a God-given claim on divine Sonship.

- Through constant assault against the soul, demonic powers have stripped many followers of Christ of consciousness concerning who they are in Christ.

- God is in a class all by Himself and He is never threatened by the exaltation of His manifest sons into their proper estate.

- The deep cry for the manifestation of the sons of God that God has built into all of creation is further proof that God is not intimidated by the entrance of the New Creation into its god-like estate (see Romans 8:19-22).

Student Class Notes:

Module
3
DEACTIVATING THE I-PROGRAM

MEMORY VERSE

"I knew you before I formed you in your mother's womb. Before you were born I set you apart and appointed you as my prophet to the nations." 6"O Sovereign Lord," I said, "I can't speak for you! I'm too young!" 7The Lord replied, "Don't say, 'I'm too young,' for you must go wherever I send you and say whatever I tell you. 8And don't be afraid of the people, for I will be with you and will protect you. I, the Lord, have spoken!" 9Then the Lord reached out and touched my mouth and said, "Look, I have put my words in your mouth! 10Today I appoint you to stand up against nations and kingdoms. Some you must uproot and tear down, destroy and overthrow. Others you must build up and plant" (Jeremiah 1:4-10).

Module OVERVIEW:

In this module we will answer the following questions:

1. What is the _____ and how does it _____ to the subject of Consciousness?
2. How does _____ the _____ "YOU" in Christ in God help you in the battle for Consciousness?

Important points to remember on this Module:

*   In Jeremiah chapter one, an interesting conversation between God and young Jeremiah ensues. What comes out of this conversation underscores the greatest hindrance to coming into a heightened state of consciousness.

*   There is a demonic program that places "self" (I) in the place where God is supposed to be.

*   This demonic program says, "I can`t," where God says, "I can!"

*   This demonic program first appeared in Lucifer and transformed him into Satan (see Isaiah 14:12-15). This "I" program is a slave of the law of sin and death.

*   Failure to break free of this demonically engineered program will doom us to a life of sin and death. This program is single handedly the greatest hindrance to living in a higher level of consciousness!

*   Many followers of Christ are wrestling with the frustration that comes from having too many unfulfilled prophecies in their lives.

*   When the Holy Spirit releases a personal prophecy over any individual the prophecy is always directed towards the "original YOU" in Christ in God!

*   The prophetic Word is the property of your regenerated human spirit not the outward man that everybody sees.

Student Class Notes:

_____

_____

_____

_____

_____

_____

_____

_____

_____

_____

_____

_____

_____

_____

_____

_____

_____

_____

_____

_____

_____

_____

_____

_____

Module
4

SHUTTING DOWN THE ENGINES OF STRESS

MEMORY VERSE

Consider the ravens, for they neither sow nor reap, which have neither storehouse nor barn; and God feeds them. Of how much more value are you than the birds? 25And which of you by worrying can add one cubit to his stature? 26If you then are not able to do the least, why are you anxious for the rest? (Luke 12:24-26, NKJV).

Module OVERVIEW:

In this module we will answer the following questions:

1. What did Jesus mean when He said, _____?

2. What is the _____?

3. Why do we live in a _____culture?

Important points to remember on this Module:

*   We live in a world that is driven by the engines of chaos and unrest.

*   In this world of chaos and unrest, people are constantly bombarded by situations that demand they enter the domain of stress.

*   According to the American Medical Journal, stress has now become the number one killer in the United States of America surpassing cancer.

*   Jesus deals a deathblow to our stress-driven culture, where worrying about tomorrow is king.

*   Yeshua admonishes us to consider the ravens, or the birds, of the air. The word "consider" literally means, to examine thoroughly.

*   Yeshua informs us that these ravens, or birds, do not sow nor reap. This is a very interesting comment because it demonstrates the advantage mankind has over the animal kingdom.

*   Yeshua tells us that our heavenly Father feeds the birds of the sky continually and none of these birds are being treated for stress at any medical facility.

Student Class Notes:

Module

5

A FALLEN KING CALLED TIME

MEMORY VERSE

To everything there is a season, a time for every purpose under heaven: 2 A time to be born, and a time to die; a time to plant, and a time to pluck what is planted; 3 a time to kill, and a time to heal; a time to break down, and a time to build up; 4 a time to weep, and a time to laugh; a time to mourn, and a time to dance; 5 a time to cast away stones, and a time to gather stones; a time to embrace, and a time to refrain from embracing; 6 a time to gain, and a time to lose; a time to keep, and a time to throw away; 7 a time to tear, and a time to sew; a time to keep silence, and a time to speak; 8 a time to love, and a time to hate; a time of war, and a time of peace (Ecclesiastes 3:1-8, NKJV).

Module OVERVIEW:

In this module will answer the following questions:

1. Why is _____in a _____?

2. Why Time was _____by God to govern and _____ mankind as it does today?

3. Why does Time _____ the _____of so many people including Citizens of the Kingdom of God?

Important points to remember on this Module:

- Before the Fall of Adam and Eve, TIME was like the womb of a woman. It was created to be the birth canal for the purposes of God.

- Time was never designed by God to govern and dominate mankind as it does today.

- TIME was simply a "spiritual womb" God created to help man "manifest in time" the finished work of God from the realms of eternity.

- The womb of TIME was never designed to bring forth demonic technologies and diabolical assignments as we see on a daily basis.

IMPORTANT DIAGRAMS

Figure: 1

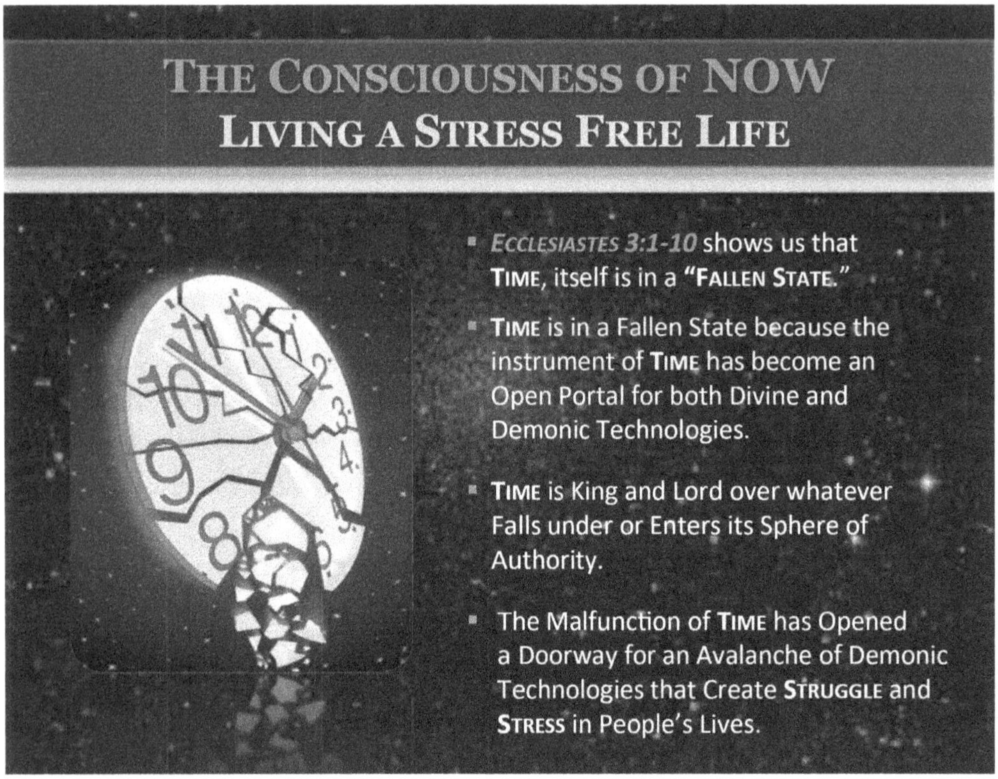

THE CONSCIOUSNESS OF NOW
LIVING A STRESS FREE LIFE

- *ECCLESIASTES 3:1-10* shows us that TIME, itself is in a "FALLEN STATE."

- TIME is in a Fallen State because the instrument of TIME has become an Open Portal for both Divine and Demonic Technologies.

- TIME is King and Lord over whatever Falls under or Enters its Sphere of Authority.

- The Malfunction of TIME has Opened a Doorway for an Avalanche of Demonic Technologies that Create STRUGGLE and STRESS in People's Lives.

Figure: 2

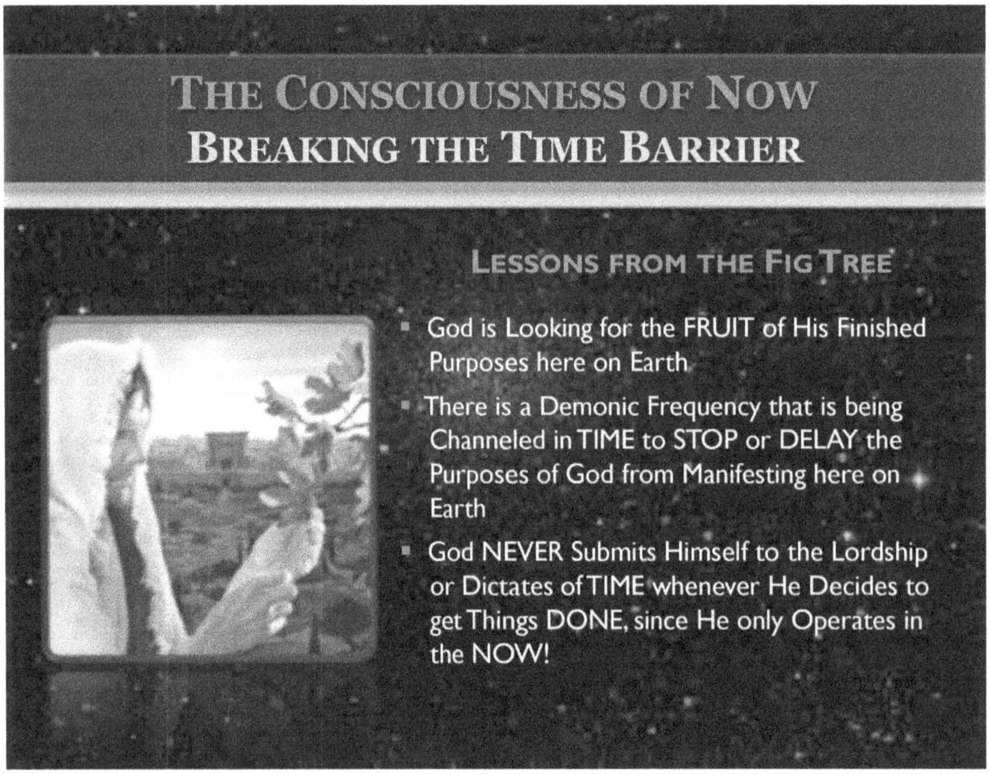

THE CONSCIOUSNESS OF NOW
BREAKING THE TIME BARRIER

LESSONS FROM THE FIG TREE

- God is Looking for the FRUIT of His Finished Purposes here on Earth.

- There is a Demonic Frequency that is being Channeled in TIME to STOP or DELAY the Purposes of God from Manifesting here on Earth

- God NEVER Submits Himself to the Lordship or Dictates of TIME whenever He Decides to get Things DONE, since He only Operates in the NOW!

Student Class Notes:

Module

6

THE GEOMETRY OF ETERNITY AND TIME

MEMORY VERSE

Now when Jesus was born in Bethlehem of Judaea in the days of Herod the king, behold, there came wise men from the east to Jerusalem, 2 Saying, Where is he that is born King of the Jews? for we have seen his star in the east, and are come to worship him. Matthew 2:1-3 (KJV)

That which hath been is now; and that which is to be hath already been; and God requireth that which is past. (Ecc 3:11-15)

Module OVERVIEW:

In this module we will answer the following questions:

1. What happens when there is an _____ of Time?

2. How did _____ know where to find the baby Jesus?

3. What's the difference between _____ and _____?

Important points to remember on this Module:

- The supernatural geometry between eternity and time will demonstrate to us the special relationship that God established between eternity and time.

- "Time" is in a fallen state but that does not in anyway diminish God's purpose for "Time" itself.

- When God created the womb of "Time" He had a clear purpose for doing so in light of His finished work in the realms of eternity.

- Our God never creates anything without a purpose because He is a God of purpose.

- Purpose is the primary motivation in the heart of God that causes Him to create.

- The revelation on the "Consciousness of NOW" will help us to profit from the supernatural alignment between eternity and time whenever God sovereignly intervenes in the affairs of men.

- The story of the Magi is a perfect example of the supernatural geometry that exists between eternity and time.

- The appearance of the Magi in the palace of King Herod to announce the supernatural birth of the King of kings represents a time of "Kairos."

IMPORTANT DIAGRAMS

Figure: 1

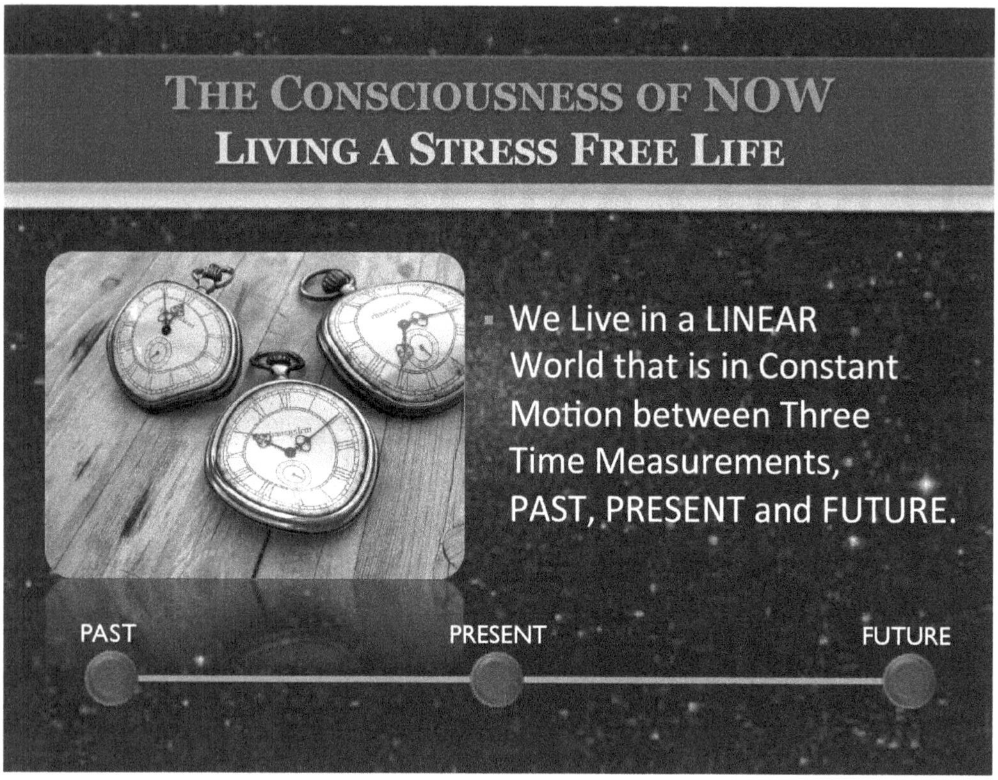

THE CONSCIOUSNESS OF NOW
LIVING A STRESS FREE LIFE

We Live in a LINEAR World that is in Constant Motion between Three Time Measurements, PAST, PRESENT and FUTURE.

PAST   PRESENT   FUTURE

Student Class Notes:

Module
7

THE CONSCIOUSNESS OF NOW: THE KEY TO STRESS FREE LIVING

MEMORY VERSE

That which hath been is now; and that which is to be hath already been; and God requireth that which is past. (Ecc 3:11-15)

He hath made every thing beautiful in his time: also he hath set the world in their heart, so that no man can find out the work that God maketh from the beginning to the end. Ecclesiastes 3:11 (KJV)

He has made everything beautiful in its time. He also has planted eternity in men's hearts and minds [a divinely implanted sense of a purpose working through the ages which nothing under the sun but God alone can satisfy], yet so that men cannot find out what God has done from the beginning to the end. Ecclesiastes 3:11 (AMP)

Module OVERVIEW:

In this module we will answer the following questions;

1. What is _____the Past?

2. What is the _____?

3. What are the five pillars of _____?

Important points to remember on this Module:
- Since the Fall of Adam the past has exercised undue influence over man's fallen nature.

- Man has now become a slave of the instrument called Time as evidenced by how much people worship the past.

- God has no measurable past or future.

- "Past" suggests that God is coming from somewhere in order to be in a place He has never been before.

- God created Time but does not live in it and neither is He defined by it.

- The only being who is excited at the prospect of us living in the past is the devil.

- The constant idolizing of the past in the hearts of the children of Israel was the reason that generation died in the Wilderness.

- "The Consciousness of Now," is critical to living a victorious life in Christ Jesus in the last days.

- The "Past" can only exert its measure of rule over us if we fail to escape the tyranny of Time continuum.

IMPORTANT DIAGRAMS

Figure: 1

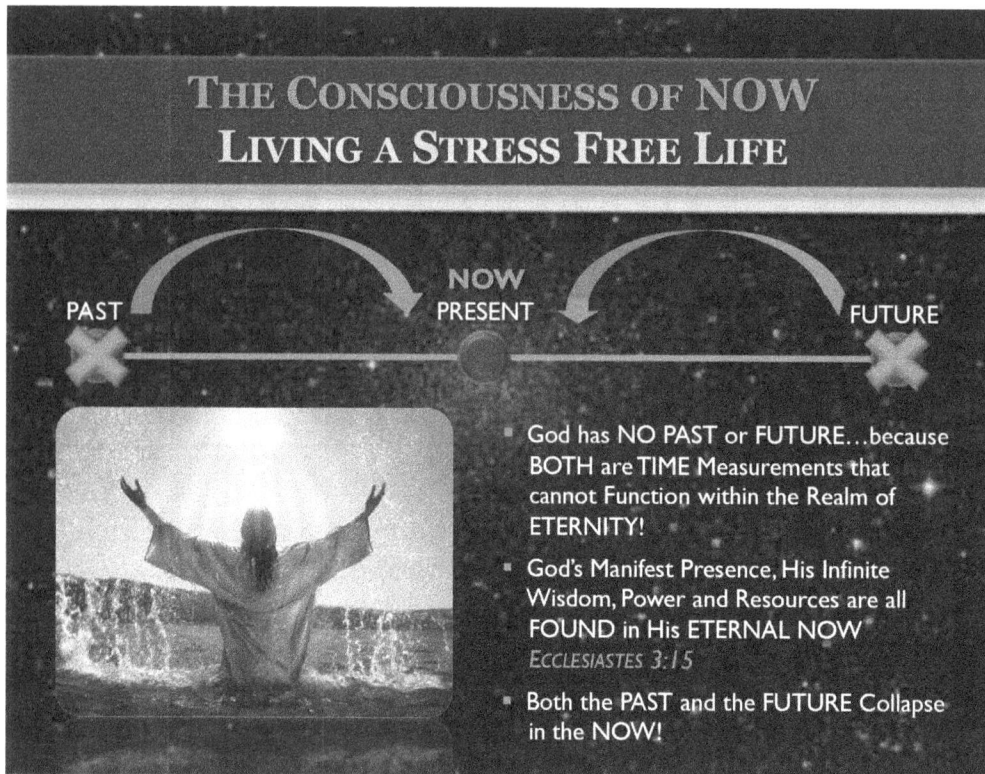

Figure: 2

IMPORTANT DIAGRAMS

Figure: 3

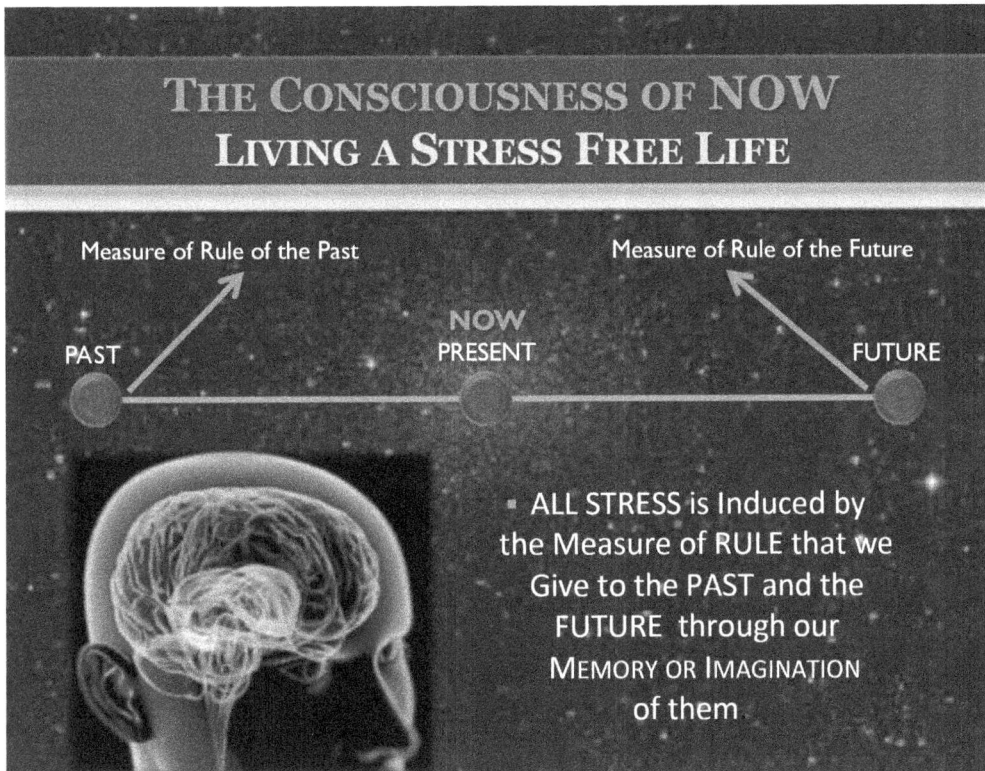

THE CONSCIOUSNESS OF NOW
LIVING A STRESS FREE LIFE

Measure of Rule of the Past

Measure of Rule of the Future

NOW
PAST   PRESENT   FUTURE

ALL STRESS is Induced by
the Measure of RULE that we
Give to the PAST and the
FUTURE through our
MEMORY OR IMAGINATION
of them

Figure: 4

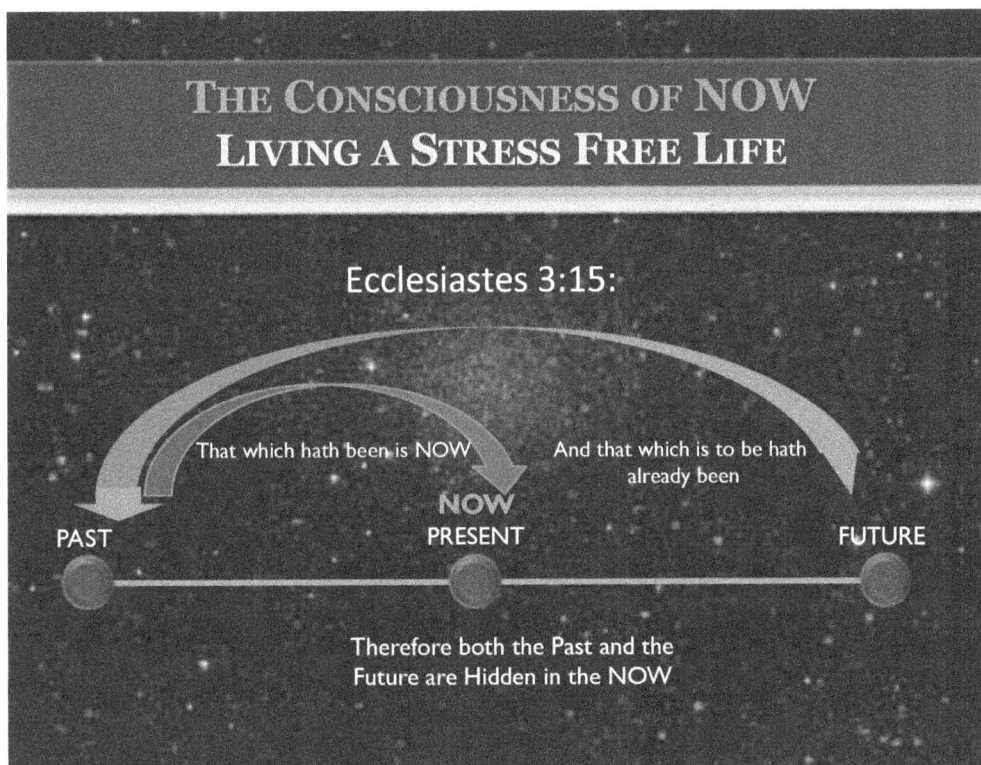

THE CONSCIOUSNESS OF NOW
LIVING A STRESS FREE LIFE

Ecclesiastes 3:15:

That which hath been is NOW   And that which is to be hath
                                     already been

NOW
PAST   PRESENT   FUTURE

Therefore both the Past and the
Future are Hidden in the NOW

Student Class Notes:

Module

8

THE HEALING OF SOUL FRAGMENTATION

MEMORY VERSE

"And when Shechem the son of Hamor the Hivite, prince of the country, saw her, he took her, and lay with her, and defiled her. And his soul cleaved unto Dinah the daughter of Jacob, and he loved the damsel, and spoke kindly unto the damsel" (Genesis 34:2-3, KJV). [Emphasis added]

Module OVERVIEW:

In this module will answer the following questions:

1. What is _____?

2. How can _____help bring about the _____of "Soul fragmentation?"

3. Why does Soul Fragmentation lead to the _____?

Important points to remember on this Module:

- Soul fragmentation is the splitting, or advanced form of compartmentalization, of a person's soul.

- Soul fragmentation is the ultimate prize sought by demonic powers.

- There is no human being who can function properly, according to God's perfect design, when his or her Soul is fragmented.

- Anything that fragments man's soul has a direct impact on his ability to realize and manifest his true self in Christ in God.

The main aim behind soul fragmentation is:

- Removal of your consciousness

- Breaking of your will

- Stripping you of your connection to God

- Creating empty slots for spirits to reside

- Evil spirit possession

IMPORTANT DIAGRAMS

Figure: 1

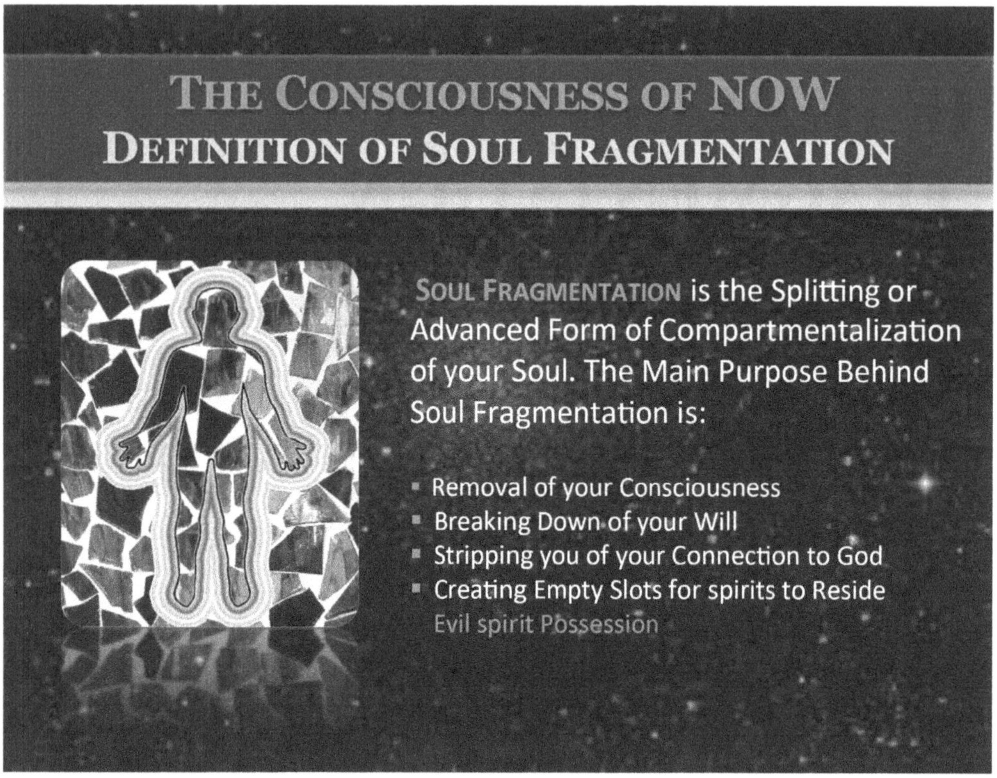

THE CONSCIOUSNESS OF NOW
DEFINITION OF SOUL FRAGMENTATION

SOUL FRAGMENTATION is the Splitting or Advanced Form of Compartmentalization of your Soul. The Main Purpose Behind Soul Fragmentation is:

- Removal of your Consciousness
- Breaking Down of your Will
- Stripping you of your Connection to God
- Creating Empty Slots for spirits to Reside
  Evil spirit Possession

Figure: 2

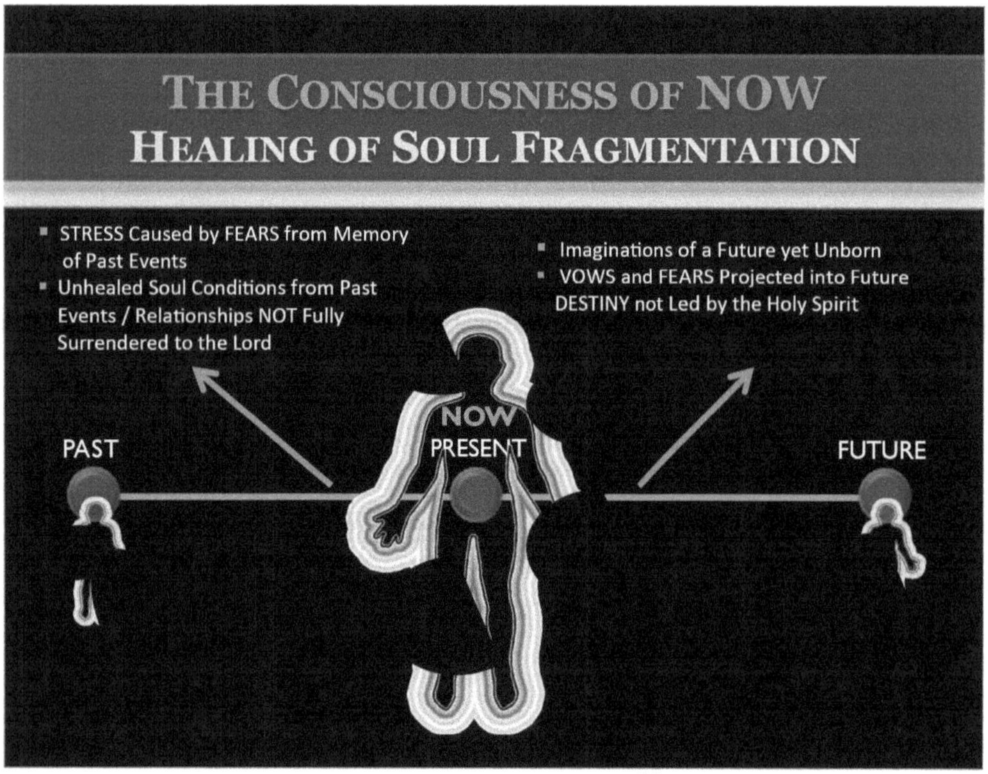

THE CONSCIOUSNESS OF NOW
HEALING OF SOUL FRAGMENTATION

- STRESS Caused by FEARS from Memory of Past Events
- Unhealed Soul Conditions from Past Events / Relationships NOT Fully Surrendered to the Lord

- Imaginations of a Future yet Unborn
- VOWS and FEARS Projected into Future DESTINY not Led by the Holy Spirit

PAST

NOW
PRESENT

FUTURE

IMPORTANT DIAGRAMS

Figure: 3

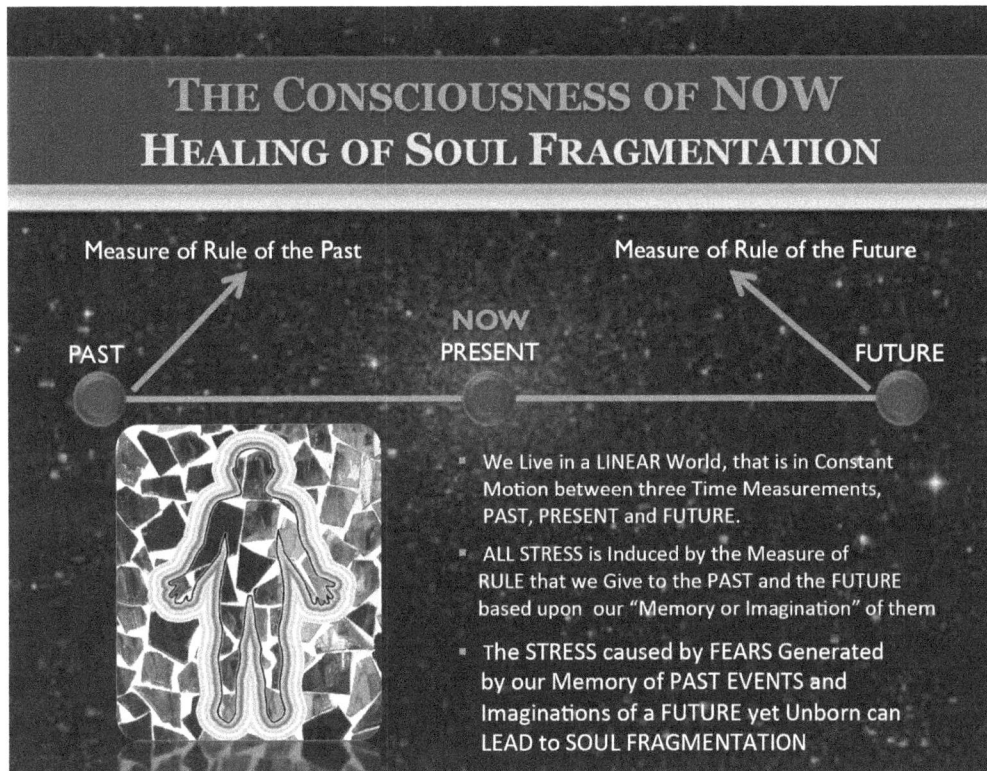

THE CONSCIOUSNESS OF NOW
HEALING OF SOUL FRAGMENTATION

Measure of Rule of the Past   Measure of Rule of the Future

PAST   NOW
                        PRESENT   FUTURE

We Live in a LINEAR World, that is in Constant Motion between three Time Measurements, PAST, PRESENT and FUTURE.

ALL STRESS is Induced by the Measure of RULE that we Give to the PAST and the FUTURE based upon our "Memory or Imagination" of them

The STRESS caused by FEARS Generated by our Memory of PAST EVENTS and Imaginations of a FUTURE yet Unborn can LEAD to SOUL FRAGMENTATION

Student Class Notes:

Module
9

BREAKING THE WITCHCRAFT OF NEEDS

MEMORY VERSE

No man can serve two masters: for either he will hate the one, and love the other; or else he will hold to the one, and despise the other. Ye cannot serve God and mammon. Matthew 6:24 (KJV)

Module OVERVIEW:

In this module we will answer the following questions:

1. What is the _____?
2. What _____ did Jesus suggest to _____our worries?

In this module we will examine:

- 'The Witchcraft of needs.' It's a demonic technology that causes people of destiny to abandon their destiny because of their felt needs.

- This technology is the source of much of the desolation that you are seeing in the Body of Christ."

- "Son, this demonic technology looks like an Octopus!"

- The "Witchcraft of needs" robs people of "God consciousness" and replaces it with "need consciousness."

- God becomes smaller in their minds while the size of their needs grew exponentially.

- This explains why so many self-proclaimed followers of Christ struggle to stay in peace.

- Their minds are completely captivated by their felt needs.

- So many followers of Christ are too busy worrying about the future to truly enjoy God's presence in the "Now!"

Student Class Notes:

Module
10
BREAKING THE TIME BARRIER

MEMORY VERSE

Behold, I am with you and will keep you wherever you go, and will bring you back to this land; for I will not leave you until I have done what I have spoken to you." 16 Then Jacob awoke from his sleep and said, "Surely the Lord is in this place, and I did not know it." Genesis 28:10-16 (NKJV)

Module OVERVIEW:

In this Module we will answer the following questions:

1. What is a _____?
2. What did _____do when he saw that _____was against him in battle?

Important points to remember on this Module:

- Death is a constant and painful reminder that we are living on borrowed "TIME."

- "TIME" has mastery over the affairs of men;

- BUT mankind was never created to serve "TIME."

- "TIME" was created to serve God and man.

- But ever since the fall of Adam and Eve "TIME" exercises great mastery over mankind.

- The prophet Amos in the ninth chapter declares, "The TIME will come," says the Lord, "when the grain and grapes will grow faster than they can be harvested."

- The only way grain and grapes can grow faster than they can be harvested is when the "TIME Barrier" between the "Seed" and "Harvest" collapses!

- When we transcend through the Spirit of God the power of "Natural law" we can break any "TIME barrier" between our seed and harvest.

IMPORTANT DIAGRAMS

Figure: 1

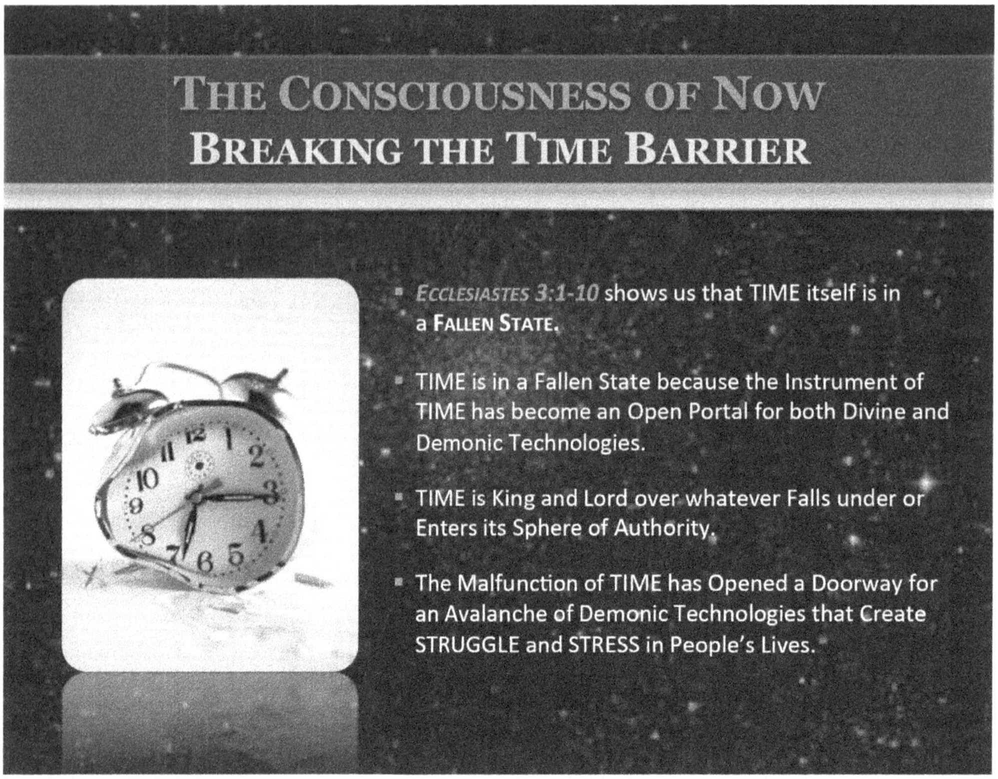

THE CONSCIOUSNESS OF NOW
BREAKING THE TIME BARRIER

- *ECCLESIASTES 3:1-10* shows us that TIME itself is in a FALLEN STATE.

- TIME is in a Fallen State because the Instrument of TIME has become an Open Portal for both Divine and Demonic Technologies.

- TIME is King and Lord over whatever Falls under or Enters its Sphere of Authority.

- The Malfunction of TIME has Opened a Doorway for an Avalanche of Demonic Technologies that Create STRUGGLE and STRESS in People's Lives.

Figure: 2

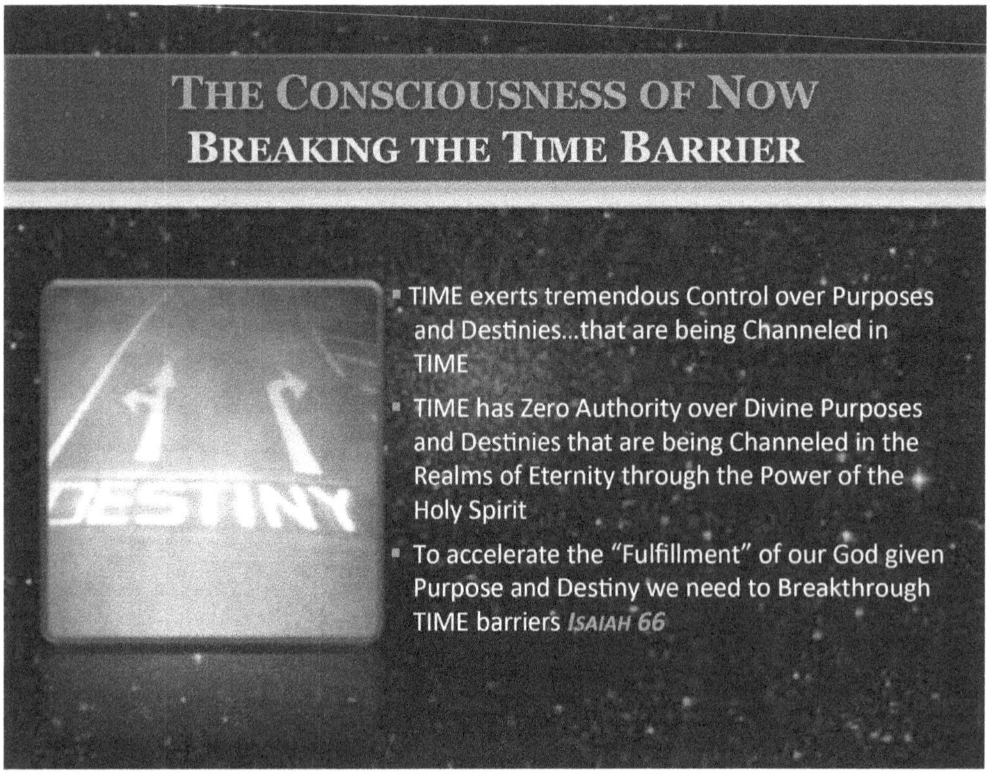

THE CONSCIOUSNESS OF NOW
BREAKING THE TIME BARRIER

- TIME exerts tremendous Control over Purposes and Destinies...that are being Channeled in TIME

- TIME has Zero Authority over Divine Purposes and Destinies that are being Channeled in the Realms of Eternity through the Power of the Holy Spirit

- To accelerate the "Fulfillment" of our God given Purpose and Destiny we need to Breakthrough TIME barriers *ISAIAH 66*

Student Class Notes:

_____

_____

_____

_____

_____

_____

_____

_____

_____

_____

_____

_____

_____

_____

_____

_____

_____

_____

_____

_____

_____

_____

_____

_____

_____

_____

Module
11

UNLEASHING YOUR CREATIVE SPIRIT

MEMORY VERSE

And the Lord came down to see the city and the tower, which the children of men builded.6And the Lord said, Behold, the people is one, and they have all one language; and this they begin to do: and now nothing will be restrained from them, which they have imagined to do (Genesis 11:5-6, KJV).

I wisdom dwell with prudence, and find out knowledge of witty inventions (Proverbs 8:12, KJV).

Module OVERVIEW:

In this module we will answer the following questions:

1. What is the knowledge of _____?
2. Why are _____supposed to be the most _____on earth?

Important points to remember on this Module:

- Living in the "Now" will affect the creativity of the Body of Christ worldwide.

- They are two thinking processes that distinguish people who are barely getting by, from people who are outrageously successful.

- These two thinking processes are deductive reasoning and creative thinking.

- Deductive reasoning is a thinking process that builds upon information that is already available to us through public domain.

- By piecing information that is readily available through public domain, most people can achieve a decent level of success.

- When young Aladdin discovered the all-mighty genie in his magic oil lamp, his life changed radically at record-speed.

- God created people with the ability to exercise their imagination.

- Unlike deductive reasoning, imagination is more often than not "out-of-the-box thinking."

- Imagination refuses to be restricted to inventions, technologies, ideas and methods of doing business that are already in the public domain.

- Great and excessive wealth awaits men and women who have awakened the "genie of their own imagination" in Christ in God.

Student Class Notes:

Module

12

THE PRIESTHOOD OF THE "NOW!"

MEMORY VERSE

For this Melchisedec, king of Salem, priest of the most high God, who met Abraham returning from the slaughter of the kings, and blessed him;2To whom also Abraham gave a tenth part of all; first being by interpretation King of righteousness, and after that also King of Salem, which is, King of peace;2Without father, without mother, without descent, having neither beginning of days, nor end of life; but made like unto the Son of God; abideth a priest continually (Hebrews 7:1-3, KJV).

Module OVERVIEW:

In this module we will answer the following questions:

1. What is the _____ of a circle that lends itself to _____?
2. Why is the _____ the priesthood of the _____?

Important points to remember on this Module:

- The only geometric figure that allows the passage of Scripture Ecclesiastes 3:15 to be true is a circle.

- In a line, the time measurements past, present and future have their own measure of rule on the consciousness of people who are trapped in this linear world.

- "Is there a priesthood that is compatible with the revelation on the "consciousness of Now"?

- Is there a priesthood that can operate accurately and comfortably in the moment could "Now"? The answer to these questions is a resounding "Yes"!

- A priesthood that is compatible with the moment called "Now" must be a priesthood that has the same mathematical properties as a circle.

- The predominant mathematical property of a circle is that it has no end or beginning.

- The Melchizedek priesthood is an everlasting priesthood God has made available to the sons of men that can align us with Him in the "Now," while infusing us with peace that surpasses all human comprehension.

Figure: 1

Student Class Notes:

OTHER BESTSELLING BOOKS FROM DR. FRANCIS MYLES
Order Your Copy Today @ www.francismyles.com

Breaking Generational Curses

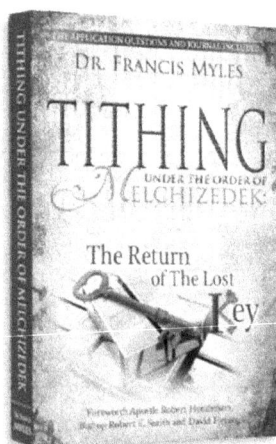

Tithing Under the Order of Melchizedek

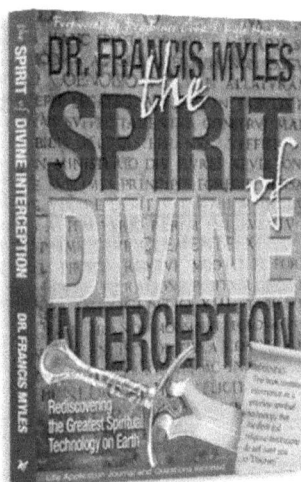

The Spirit of Divine Interception

www.ingramcontent.com/pod-product-compliance
Lightning Source LLC
Chambersburg PA
CBHW081141090426
42736CB00018B/3432